CHANGING TOOLS

MATT BOULTON

Matt Boulton knows that when people are stuck, the last thing they need to hear is psychology-speak or some complicated theory. People want a simple way to understand what went wrong and how to fix it. When it comes to their own healing, people need to be in the driver's seat and deserve a process which is simple enough for them to feel confident and in control.

Matt's own story is one of finding reconciliation after a painful separation, and restoration from the life-controlling habits which brought it about. He has gleaned a wealth of experience working with people from all walks of life in his thirteen years as a counsellor. Matt combines this with an easy-to-follow style in Changing Tools to get you on the road to finding real, lasting change.

CHANGING TOOLS

www.mattboulton.com

First Edition ©2013

Changing Tools

ISBN: 978-0-9923721-0-1

Lightning Source

Scoresby, Victoria.

All rights reserved. Distribution or duplication of this material in whole or in part, without the express permission of the author is strictly prohibited.

Cover: Graphic Design, Tamar Petersen, Red Box Studios, www.redboxstudios.com.au
Formatting: Red Box Studios

Dedicated to the memory of
Michael Bruce Osbourne (1966-2009) who
was generous with his skills and any tools he
stumbled upon that could help others.

CONTENTS

Introduction   6

1. Identifying the Tools   11

2. Naming the Cost   19

3. Revisiting the First Discovery   29

4. The Cost of Feeling Normal   41

5. What Are You Looking For?   49

6. Engaging the Alternative   67

INTRODUCTION

A tree saw - that's the only instrument Dr Payne ever carried; the only one he ever needed. To the folks of Nyevia, he was the island's only brain surgeon. Sure, it was well known that his procedures usually produced more than their fair share of blood and gore. If patients were lucky enough to recover, their recovery would always be a long and difficult ordeal. Persistent infection and lifelong profound scarring were almost taken as a given but, for Dr Payne's patients, he was their only hope and last resort.

For 14 years Dr Payne would have his successes and failures, and no one could dispute that he was improving over time as he became more skilled in the delicate use of the tree saw. He was, in fact, a master of the art; perhaps the world's finest tree saw-wielding surgeon of all time.

At first, when he began to hear reports from the other islands about the use of the "scalpel," Dr Payne was sceptical. After all, how could such a tiny instrument really have the muscle for brain surgery? And how long might it take to train himself from scratch in the use of a new tool? How could it be worth throwing away all those years of being the best at something? Surely it was better to stick with what he knew, and not allow some passing fad to complicate things?

The first time Dr Payne succumbed to using a scalpel, he didn't even realise he had made an incision. Where was all the blood which usually accompanied this kind of work, he wondered? It seemed all too easy, and he could see that stitching was going to be a dream.

Before long he also noticed a few other changes. Wounds were healing a whole lot quicker than before, and infection was now a rarity. Patients reported less scarring than they might have expected. Survival rates became a pleasant surprise.

"This scalpel thing," mused Dr Payne, "could really take off."

I'm sure it would come as no surprise to learn that Dr Payne never did return to his trusty tree saw. Like you, I and the majority of the human race, Dr Payne tended to avoid any extra work which did not produce a positive outcome. He also avoided inconvenience unless it was absolutely necessary, and pain unless it was producing some kind of profit (his own pain that is).

That's why Dr Payne was initially not interested in adopting this new "scalpel"; because doing anything new always involves some degree of inconvenience, new work, and often pain.

As a twelve-year-old boy, I used to enjoy working on my bike - tightening the nuts, adjusting the brakes, and generally trying to keep it maintained the best way I knew how.

I had an old shifting spanner which was good for just about everything, since I could just keep adjusting it to fit each and every nut; from the large ones on the wheels right through to the tiny nuts on the brake cables.

At times it was frustrating that the shifter kept slipping off the nuts, scarring my knuckles and putting rounded edges on the nuts. But as far as I knew, this was the tool for each and every job.

Like Dr Payne, I was not looking for another tool. I was happy enough with what I had.

One day a teenage neighbour who was more mechanically savvy asked me why I was not using a spanner. I can still remember his words to this day: "You don't dig a hole with a teaspoon when you can use a shovel." I reluctantly tried using a set of spanners, and have never looked back.

That day I learned a valuable lesson about myself and about human nature: we will continue to use any tool which is working for us, even if it is not the right tool, and even if it may be causing other problems for us or those around us.

What about you? If you take a moment to stop and think, can you identify any broken or blunt tools which you keep picking up?

Do you have any habits or behaviours which continue to cause problems for you, and yet you somehow continue to pick them up again and again? Some of us might even be wondering whether we will ever be able to be free of our particular troublesome tools.

For some, a blunt tool might be an addiction which helps us cope with a lot of internal pain we are going through.

For others, a blunt tool might be a relationship we are using to feel secure, or even a person we are taking too much responsibility for because it makes us feel like a "good person" when we help them.

Sometimes rage or abuse can be the tools which people reach for in order to be heard, respected or taken seriously. For some, obsessive-compulsive, anxious or controlling traits can be the levers they use in an attempt to feel in control of some small part of their own "out of control" world.

For many of us, a blunt tool may have been the best tool a parent had to hand down to us. Some become family heirlooms, faithfully handed down from generation to generation.

For some of us, the tool may have just been something which we desperately grabbed for during a pressured or traumatic moment; perhaps when we were too young to know how to respond in the way that a rational adult might do.

The really good news I hope to convey is that irrespective of how blunt or broken your tools are, what type or shape they come in, and where you found and first picked them up, the same key principle applies to you as to everybody else:

When you at last find the best tool for the job, you will never return to the old tool, since doing so would only be choosing to accept something unnecessary and inconvenient.

Just like Dr Payne, your innate human bias towards laziness is not only your problem; it will also turn out to be your saviour. We are not only too lazy, but also too clever to continue using a redundant tool.

The truth is, you have not yet discovered the best tool for each and every problem, situation and relationship which you are going to encounter. There are better tools out there waiting to be found, picked up and trusted.

The question is, how will you know when you have found them? This book is about knowing where to look for better tools, how to recognise them when you find them, and what your broken and blunt tools can teach you about yourself.

10 | CHANGING TOOLS

1.
IDENTIFYING THE TOOLS

You are not your problem. Your problem is your problem.

If you've ever called yourself an alcoholic, a procrastinator, an addict, an abuser, a liar, a cheat, a quitter or worse, then you are already walking down the road of disempowerment. The very moment you choose to accept a label, you have just begun making one of your tools into an extension of your personality.

Think about that for a moment. It's reasonable for a chef to call himself a chef, but once he starts referring to himself as a knife, a rolling pin or another one of his tools, we can see that something is very wrong with his mental state. Your tools should never define you and they should never own you.

Chances are, you did not come into the world with your own particular blunt and broken tools, but you picked them up along the way and began to use them.

Eric Berne in his classic work on human interactions, "Games People Play," describes a game he calls "Wooden Leg" (Berne, 1964, p.162). This is a game some people play (or a way of relating to others) as a means of avoiding responsibility, and it works by constantly reminding other people of some particular handicap with which we have labelled ourselves. When questioned about our actions, or inaction, our retort will be, "What can you expect me to do, since I have a wooden leg?"

If you have chosen to define yourself by a label, it is likely that you are unconsciously playing a good old-fashioned game of Wooden Leg. Like all games that we consistently play, there is always a payoff, something you must gain from playing the game. In this case, the payoff is the avoidance of at least some of the responsibility for your own behaviour:

"I can't help myself. I'm just a control freak."

"I just have a short fuse."

"I know I'm a bad mother."

In all of these cases, the subtext is something like, "Don't expect too much from me." Labels have the ability to do that. They remove a measure of responsibility for our behaviour by saying that our broken tool is just a part of us, and they serve to get other people's disappointment out of the way.

Whilst it may seem like an act of humility to acknowledge one of our weaknesses, the truth is that our self-labelling is often a veiled way of saying, "Yes, I'm disappointed in the person I am too, but what can I do?"

When somebody has a real disability, people don't question it for fear of appearing rude. In the same way there is often something untouchable about the label you adopt, and people would feel very rude if they were to question it. But you are not a label; you are someone who learned that labelling yourself could save you from some hard work, inconvenience or pain.

Since labelling ourselves is the first blunt tool we need to confront in order to start moving forward, let's unpack this tool a little more.

When we feel guilt, it tells us that we have done something wrong and that we may need to acknowledge and make amends for something before we can move on. There is short-term pain and hard work involved with most guilt.

Shame, on the other hand, tells us that there is something inadequate about us or that something is wrong with us. For that reason, shame is a lot more personal, a lot more weighty, and usually makes us want to withdraw or even hide ourselves from other people.

If we are in the business of collecting labels about ourselves, we cannot do that without taking on some corresponding shame message. Remember, shame is heavy to carry around, and exposure to its toxicity is always harmful. Like arsenic, small doses of it can accumulate in our system over time until critical levels begin to kill us.

Your tools should never define you and they should never own you

The "bad mother" tag is a good example of a popular label, possibly employed to overstate the case and hopefully elicit sympathy and even a little positive support. Whilst it may be a short-term deflector for responsibility, "bad mother" is a weighty and shameful label to have to bear.

Rather than using the "bad mother" label and accumulating more shame, it may be better in the long term to accept some helpful short-term guilt in order to move quickly through the pain: "I should have remembered to pack a jumper for my kids, but I got it wrong. I'm not a bad mother but I did make a mistake, which I can learn from."

We all make mistakes all of the time. They are part of our humanity, and do not require us to play games or define ourselves by some new label in order to cope. If we do choose to pick up a label, then we pick up and ingest something toxic.

Your blunt and broken tools are not a part of you. They are something separate from you which you unfortunately sometimes choose to pick up and use.

Like a qualified tradesperson, or Dr Payne, you may have become very competent in the use of your blunt or broken tools. But there is a major difference. Whereas it is rare to find a tradesperson who could not at least name every tool in their toolbox, most of us have very little insight into the tools we use every day in our lives and relationships.

John was a big, burly Islander who presented to me for anger management. In the course of our discussions, we agreed that his anger was only an emotion, but his habit of picking up and using violence as his tool of choice was causing problems for him and for other people.

As John shared more of his story, other patterns of behaviour began to appear like recurring themes. Before he had completed two sessions of therapy, John had already identified a whole range of blunt tools which he had been using for a very long time.

Next he began to name them out loud: "Alcohol, women, rescuing people, running away, withdrawing, and violence." I could see that for John, as for most people, recognising his regular use of blunt and broken tools for the first time was becoming quite liberating, if daunting.

Over several weeks, John and I would sit with his blunt and broken tools depicted on sheets of paper and spread out all over the floor. As one would call for his attention, I would ask him to pick it up and hold it. Having it now safely outside of himself, he was free to put it down, pick it up, engage with it and fully unpack it in a whole new way.

John was a good man, and it's true that he had many character strengths and even a whole range of effective tools, which we were not talking about, for life and relationships. He was also quite a resourceful man who had searched for tools in order to cope with his own particular circumstances and to help him to "get through."

Like Dr Payne, his tools were only somewhat effective and, although they were also causing him damage, they were still the best tools he had been able to find.

If you were to put aside your tools of distraction for long enough to sit quietly and focus, I wonder if you would also find a few blunt and broken tools which you continue to use.

I wonder if you would be able to name them accurately without naming or labelling yourself. If you were brave enough to write them down on paper, for only yourself to see, like John you would be able to begin engaging with them in a way which you have never done before.

On the following page there is some space for you to begin recording your thoughts and listing the dysfunctional tools you would like to engage with. This is the first of a number of response panels which you will be asked to fill in. Please make the most of these, since they are intended to be your chapter-by-chapter companion as you begin retooling your life and relationships.

If you don't like writing in books, I would encourage you to use a separate sheet of paper or a personal journal. Whichever way you do it, the saying is as true as when it was first said more than 2000 years ago: "The truth shall set you free."

Can you sit with the truth long enough until it does?

NAME THE TOOL:

LIST THE DYSFUNCTIONAL TOOLS
YOU WOULD LIKE TO ADDRESS:

_____

_____

_____

_____

_____

_____

_____

_____

_____

_____

_____

_____

_____

_____

_____

_____

_____

_____

_____

18 | CHANGING TOOLS

2.
NAMING THE COST

It has been said that healing comes when the pain of remaining as we are becomes greater than the pain involved in changing.

While the process of change and healing is not quite as simple as that, it is still a very motivating exercise for you to take stock of everything your blunt and broken tools are costing you.

Brad was in no doubt that his use of "abusive vengeance" whenever he felt unloved had already cost him two marriages, quite a few friendships, his house, access to his children, and perhaps the most part of his reputation.

Think about that for a moment. Can you think of any kind of tool which you would allow to cost you that much? The strange thing is, Brad can hate his "abusive vengeance" all he likes for what it has already cost him but, to this day, he has still not been able to put this tool down, despite all of the profound damage to his personal world.

Of course, it should not be a surprise that hating our blunt and broken tools is not enough to make us abandon them. Ask any drug user what their habit has cost them, and you will see that Brad is not alone in finding himself stuck with something he hates. Go along to any Gamblers or Alcoholics Anonymous meeting and you will find that there is no lack of hatred for the habits that are costing people so much in their lives and relationships.

At some stage though, we need to come to the realisation that the negative results of using our tools are never enough in themselves to make us put them down, since they have nothing at all to do with why we first picked them up.

> *...it should not be a surprise that hating our blunt and broken tools is not enough to make us abandon them*

If you have some dysfunctional tools which you would like to be able to get rid of, then I'm sure you already have some sense of what they have cost you.

In fact, of all the people who have presented to me for therapy over the years, almost all of them have this one thing in common: an understanding that their dysfunction is costing them something. Without that personal insight, it would be unusual for someone to seek counselling in the first place.

The mistake, then, is to think that the cost of dysfunction in itself would be enough to make us able to change.

What coming to a greater understanding of the costs does is create in us a greater hunger for change, produce a greater resolve to do something, and set us in the direction of searching out new tools.

One such weary traveller was Josh, a young man who continued to pick up and use alcohol as a tool.

Although it was difficult to imagine this quiet and shy computer geek getting into any kind of trouble, Josh was soon to face court on a charge of grievous bodily harm to another night-clubber following another one of his drunken outings.

In this case, it is very obvious that the cost of using the dysfunctional tool is what has brought the young man to seek counselling. He is acutely aware that his habit is quite likely to cost him some jail time, or at least a hefty fine, but he has so far been unable to put this damaging tool down.

It is not until he is able to sit in my office and literally hold the word "alcohol" outside of himself that he is able to fully realise all that it has cost him.

Josh begins to remember that he has lost the respect of quite a few people who mattered to him, and has lost several friendships as a result. His relationship with his girlfriend, who he had hoped to marry, has also deteriorated as a result of his drinking, and is now possibly coming to an end.

He remembers the pressure that his drinking has brought upon his work life as well as the opportunities for promotion he has lost over his time with the company.

Suddenly he becomes aware that his drinking has not only cost him hundreds of dollars every fortnight, but his dreams of owning his own home have been put on hold as a result.

When Josh gets really honest, he shares how his use of alcohol has cost him a great deal of confidence and self-esteem.

If you are also prepared to spend some time focussing on your own dysfunctional tools, then you too can gain a deeper insight into their true costs to you and those you love.

Using the response panel at the end of this chapter, take the time to note down some of the "negatives" or costs of the tool you are engaging with. Like Josh, you will gain a greater awareness of the cost of maintaining your own broken tools, and become even more determined in your resolve to find better ones.

The following list will help you identify specific costs across the following areas:

FINANCIAL / MATERIAL COSTS

Many of the blunt or broken tools which we continue to pick up and use come with a clear and direct financial cost (eg. alcohol, gambling, cigarettes). For some other tools, the financial costs may be indirect or hidden (eg. missing work days, being overlooked for promotion, or having to repair things you have broken).

Since change is annoying and inconvenient, it's quite likely that you might be in denial about the absolute financial costs of maintaining your dysfunctional tools, so you may need to sit with this one for a little longer and explore it a little deeper before moving on.

I suggest noting any financial costs in terms of weekly costs, monthly costs and annual costs; that is, note each cost in all three ways. When you see the cost of maintaining your dysfunctional tools across a whole year, you may be very surprised by what you find (eg. $40 carton of beer per week = $173.33 per month = $2080 per year).

Once you have expressed your costs in all three ways, stop and consider the opportunity cost of your dysfunctional tool. The opportunity cost is the real material cost of what you are missing out on as a result of the financial cost of your dysfunctional tool (eg. $2080 per year = the cost of a ski trip, a home cinema, or a fancy new wardrobe).

Where possible, just like Josh did, express the opportunity cost in terms of your own dreams and what is important to you.

TIME COSTS

Our dysfunctional tools often rob us of our time. Simon was a young married man who was "stressed out" by the demands of his university course, and was using online gaming as his tool for coping. Each night he was spending about five hours on the computer, losing hours of sleep, quality time with his wife, and time he could be studying in order to reduce his "study stress."

As with the financial costs, it will help you to note down your lost time in weekly, monthly and annual terms, as well as in terms of other lost opportunities.

Remember, you are never "spending" your time. As with your money, you are always investing it. You can invest your time or your money in constructive ways, which will bring you long-term satisfaction, or you can invest it in short-term pleasure or tools for "coping."

To say that you are wasting your time, spending it, or watching it slip through your fingers is just another way of avoiding responsibility for the impulsive way in which you might be investing your time.

Sadly, the difference with our time is that, unlike money, we can never have it back again.

PHYSICAL COSTS

Often there is a physical cost to maintaining blunt or broken tools. Again, some are direct and obvious, and others may be indirect.

When taking stock of the physical costs of your dysfunctional tools, it's important to get beyond generalised descriptions (eg. "I know these cigarettes are doing me harm") and to be as specific as you can (eg. "These cigarettes are the reason why I cough up muck every morning, they are making my asthma worse and are bringing me closer to cancer, heart disease and an earlier death than I deserve").

Remember, because change is inconvenient, denial is going to give you a fight and tempt you to minimise and generalise physical costs in a way that "doesn't sound so bad really."

MENTAL / EMOTIONAL COSTS

Many of the dysfunctional tools which people maintain and continue to use have a mental or emotional cost attached. Some of these might include anxiety, depression, fear, suicidal ideations, shame, grief, paranoia, obsessive thoughts, compulsive behaviours, panic attacks, numbness, or a sense of being outside of yourself looking in.

Since a good number of mental and emotional problems also lead to physical symptoms, you should also include on your list things like migraines, insomnia, rashes, abdominal upsets, ulcers, reflux, heartburn, obesity, hyperarousal, neck and shoulder tension etc.

SOCIAL / RELATIONAL COSTS

Since dysfunctional tools are often antisocial in nature, they can also cost us in terms of relationships and social contact. David was a dad, with a two-year-old son, whose wife was very unhappy about him spending five hours per night playing a shoot-em-up network game over the Internet, and letting his family responsibilities go by the wayside. When she finally gave him an ultimatum, he chose to leave the family home and be separated from his wife and son rather than to put his game down and come to bed.

When it comes to the relational costs which people will pay in order to hold onto their blunt and broken tools, truth really is stranger than fiction. No doubt there are people in your own circle of friends who have lost a marriage or two for the sake of their dysfunctional tools.

The negative results of using our tools are never enough in themselves to make us put them down, since they have nothing at all to do with why we first picked them up

As you count the cost of maintaining your own tools, remember to count the relational cost across your lifetime, not just in the recent past. Be sure to include friends and family who have lost respect for you or cut you off, and those who you have abandoned or had a strained relationship with.

Since many of our dysfunctional tools cause us to feel shame and to hide ourselves, you should not forget to include your own withdrawal and isolation. This may even be another tool, which you might like to unpack separately.

MORAL / SPIRITUAL COSTS

When we know we are picking up tools which go against our own personal values, the damage to our own moral compass can be a heavy price to pay. When we know our integrity is being compromised, it is normal to feel shame and to begin asking ourselves moral questions such as, "What kind of person would do this?" or "What have I become?"

If the tool you are picking up is against your beliefs or your religious faith, you will probably find that you draw back from God and from others in your faith community. This can be a devastating experience, since you can feel cut off from the very things that are most important and central to your life and worldview.

If you have enjoyed a close relationship with God in the past, you may begin to identify as a "backslider" and even wallow in your own personal world of pain and failure. In the Christian faith, the Bible is clear that our response at these times should be to run towards God and our church, not away from them, and not to wait until we feel "clean" from our shame.

LEGAL COSTS

If your particular dysfunctional tools are causing you problems with the law or with litigation, you should make note of these costs too.

As with the other cost centres, you should be as specific as possible and include indirect results of these costs. For example, if it is likely that you will be fined, you should include the financial repercussions and opportunity costs of being fined. If it is likely that you will be imprisoned, you should detail all of the social, financial, and other costs of being locked away.

If you are serious about changing your life, I'm going to suggest that you don't quickly move on to the next chapter. You only get one chance to follow the whole process through for the first time, so why not do it as well as you possibly can? Respect yourself and spend as long as it takes to thoroughly work through all of the negative aspects and costs of your dysfunctional tools.

Remember, change only comes when the inconvenience of staying the same becomes greater than the inconvenience of the change itself. Since you need to be thoroughly convinced that the change is going to be worth it, you need to paint as realistic an account of the current costs as you possibly can.

This is especially important because it's likely that, at this stage, you don't even know what you will be exchanging your dysfunctional tools for.

You need to work against the strong forces of denial just to hate your current situation enough to go looking for new tools. That's certainly going to take more motivation than you've had in the past, so promise yourself that you are not going to cut corners this time.

Put the work in to complete counting the cost before you move on to chapter three.

NAME THE TOOL:

NEGATIVE

WHAT NEGATIVE EFFECTS IS THIS TOOL HAVING ON YOU?

CHANGING TOOLS

3.
REVISITING THE FIRST DISCOVERY

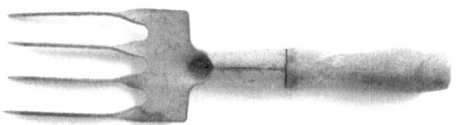

When I first met Nigel in the waiting room of the counselling centre, I have to admit that I was more than a little intimidated.

From head to toe, there was barely an inch of real estate where Nigel did not bear an aggressive looking tattoo, except perhaps in the places where elaborate body piercings were jangling about. He was an impressive and fearsome looking man; you would have to have a death-wish to cross him deliberately.

Ironically, over time I would learn that not only was Nigel one of the most tender-hearted people I had ever met, he was also one of the most frightened.

If there was even a sudden sound, such as the air-conditioner changing cycles, Nigel would almost jump out of his skin. He was one of the clients who taught me to always announce if I was about to stand up to grab a book or a pen and paper. That's because Nigel was a Vietnam veteran with a serious case of Post-Traumatic Stress Disorder.

He had his own word for the tattoos and piercings adorning so much of his body. They were his "armour," and he confided that they were his way of keeping people at a safe distance, since he had been so seriously hurt in past relationships, and had the world taken out from under him by the terrors of war.

It's hard to find a better example of a tool being implemented so effectively. Nigel's basic need to cope and feel safe in his world has required him to find something to prevent people from getting too close to him. Whatever we might think about the way he has chosen to do it, we have to admire and respect his ingenuity in finding a tool which is able to do just what is required.

But where do we learn to pick up tools like that? Who or what teaches us the amazing resourcefulness which sees us through to survival in a world that we would otherwise be helpless to cope with? There are probably as many answers to that question as there are battlers reaching for the tools to cope.

Over the years I have noticed that we do tend to go looking in similar kinds of places for effective tools.

Of course, the most empowering question for you to answer will be about where you first learned to pick up the faulty tools which are relevant to you.

INSTINCT AND IMPULSE:

Like animals, we human beings have a section of our brains which is dedicated to giving an automatic response to pain, danger or threat, and it does so at lightning speed. Since the amygdala sits at the base of the brain and the top of the spinal cord, no conscious thought is required before it causes your whole body to quickly respond to a thumb tack on your chair or a burn from the hot plate.

Between the amygdala and the cerebral cortex (where conscious rational thought occurs) is the limbic system.

This part of your brain develops significantly as you grow into adulthood, and I like to think of it as the "brakes" of the brain, since it is largely responsible for impulse control. When you are very small and your limbic system is undeveloped, it is very difficult for you to put the brakes on your emotions and to think things through. You simply react impulsively most of the time.

Depending on your stage of growth and development, threatening situations, fear, risk or trauma will produce differing responses from the working together of the amygdala (engine room), the developing limbic system (the brakes), and the cerebral cortex (the filing and sorting system, which makes sense of things).

You may be familiar with the concept of a "fight or flight" response. Depending on the seriousness of the threat, you are more likely to instinctively reach for fighting tools if you are older and tools of flight if you are younger. If you are very young and/or profoundly intimidated, it is likely that you will neither fight nor flee, but freeze.

All three groups of responses are important to us and will cause us to reach for different types of coping tools, many of which we will continue to use for far too long.

Gina was a young Aboriginal woman whose marriage had become stuck in several different areas. When she came to counselling with her husband Phil, they would both talk about their children, their life and their church quite happily. But from time to time, when an issue would arise which was even just a bit confronting, a remarkable thing would happen. A silence would fall upon Gina like a cloak, her gaze would drop to the ground and no question, direct or indirect, could elicit another response from her. She would be totally frozen and utterly unreachable.

It would emerge that Gina had been a foster child from a very young age after her mother's use of violence and alcohol had shaken her little world and ultimately resulted in her removal. Because she had first encountered serious physical abuse at such a young age, the tools she had reached for had been those of freezing.

> *Who or what teaches us the amazing resourcefulness which sees us through to survival in a world that we would otherwise be helpless to cope with?*

Since the threat of her drunken abusive mother was too overpowering to fight or even run from, her brain's amazing resilience and resourcefulness produced a survival response something like: "If I say nothing and do nothing, she will eventually stop and return to normal."

On one level, we have to concede that this was an effective tool, since it probably kept her alive. Nevertheless, as an adult who had never been able to replace her freezing tools, Gina found herself utterly incapable of coping with even the ups and downs of a normal marriage.

Although I have said that these kinds of freezing responses from adults are remarkable, they are certainly not uncommon.

Remember Simon, the married student who would sit in front of the computer playing games for hours every night instead of going to bed with his unhappy wife? In therapy Simon was usually quietly spoken but, when things got really confronting, he would tear up, cower like a little boy, and the quietest timid little voice would come forth from his lips.

As a child, Simon had picked up these tools to cope with repeated physical and sexual abuse from a friend who his family had trusted. Like many others, his freezing tools were now robbing him of the ability to gain a job, go to bed with his wife or work through any uncomfortable discussion.

Thankfully, though, he was progressing ever so slightly with each session as he slowly learned to sit with his overwhelming sense of fear and insecurity.

When Tony became the victim of systematic abuse at the hands of his school masters, he was old enough to want to hurt them back. But for better or worse, his limbic system was developed enough to be able to put the brakes on this fighting response, so his higher-order thinking could reason that this would lead him to much greater trouble with the boarding school and his parents. What the limbic system could not do, however, was put the brakes on him fantasising about it; even wishing that God would punish his offenders.

As an adult, he has lost two marriages due largely to his own latent aggression and abusiveness. Despite attempts to reconcile with his ex-wife, his continuing moments of impulsivity and verbal berating have probably sabotaged any chance he had.

In "Games People Play," Eric Berne describes a game he calls "Now I've Got You, Son of a Bitch" (Berne, 1964, p.87). This is a game favoured by those of us who first picked up our coping tools during the fighting stage. Since my own disempowerment occurred during that time (later primary school), I must admit that this silly game has caused me moments of great immaturity on the road, where childish contests have been played out with other drivers.

It is probably also the reason why one of my good friends, Troy, will tell you that litigation is one of his favourite hobbies. He simply loves taking people to court - either on behalf of himself or of somebody powerless - and seeing them brought to justice. It's a real hobby, and no doubt an extension of the powerless teenage years he spent with a violent and abusive father.

It's probably also no surprise that both Troy and myself have carried the fight into our respective marriages. As the result of our own aggression and domestic violence, both of us have been separated from our wives at some stage.

With those years behind me, my 13 years of working with and counselling domestic violence perpetrators has shown me again and again that, in conflict, those of us who choose the fighting tools will generally tend to exhaust all of them before we will ever back down.

If you're married to someone like that, it's worth thinking about that worsening trend very soberly, since denial can literally be a killer. Make no mistake about it, without proper intervention of some kind, abusive relationships will continue to follow a worsening trend and will almost always end with a separation, divorce, homicide or suicide.

For me, that separation 20 years ago was a wake-up call. It was a clear sign to me that I needed to find new tools, and find them fast. Since any kind of relapse was utterly unacceptable and the stakes far too high, it would take another ten months for my wife and I to gain the confidence to consider living together again.

> *For men in particular, anger can be quite an effective shield to keep other people at a distance*

It would take time to sit for 13 weeks in a men's perpetrator group. It would take time to talk and pray with my few church friends who knew what was really going on. It took time to do the hard yards of couple counselling so that our future hope could have some real substance, rather than just a "fingers crossed" approach.

Whatever your blunt tools, your change will take time too, and it's more than likely that it will involve other people helping you. Are you angry? A fighter? This too is a tool, and often a tool for avoiding emotions which are more difficult to sit with.

Have you ever been really angry with someone, but when you were all alone, you eventually just broke down and cried about it? Chances are the pain was always there, but like Nigel with his own particular brand of armour, you let anger form a barrier between you and the person causing you hurt. It's safer that way.

For men in particular, anger can be quite an effective shield to keep other people at a distance.

Think about this: if you jump out from behind a door and scare a woman, she is likely to scream. Scare a man and he may hit you, face up, or yell at you.

Why is that? It's because men will often use anger as a shield for covering fear. If they do it in these kinds of practical situations, we should not be surprised if some men also respond with anger when they feel scared or insecure in relationships.

So far we still have not addressed the instinctive response which we might call a "flight response." This response arises from a perceived need to run, retreat or escape from a perceived threat.

In relationships, this is often expressed as a withdrawal from or avoidance of somebody. In its physical form, it is not too difficult to identify, since it usually involves somebody getting up and leaving, separating or even literally running away.

For example, following a divorce or separation, some dads really struggle to deal with the emotional depth, negotiation or compromise which their new custody or access arrangements may bring about. One common response is to make no effort in an attempt to avoid their ex-partner altogether. I think you would agree that this is a very costly tool for avoiding having to deal with an uncomfortable situation.

You might recall that our big burly Islander friend John had identified "running away" as one of his tools for coping with relational problems. When John would make a mess of something (or perhaps get somebody pregnant), he would literally just run away to another country and start again, leaving behind a new trail of destruction.

This kind of physical flight response is a lot more common than you may expect. Many couples have reported to me that they have been finding it difficult to communicate with each other because they are always working or busy with other activities. In fact, more often than not, the truth is that they are always working or busy with other activities because they are finding it difficult or uncomfortable to communicate.

Even more common is the use of emotional withdrawal, where people are physically present but emotionally checked out. Technology can be a great aid to those looking for a tool to remove themselves emotionally. As Jonathan Safran Foer suggests, "Technology celebrates connectedness, but encourages retreat" (Safran Foer, 2013).

Even more common is the use of emotional withdrawal, where people are physically present, but emotionally checked out.

Do you know someone who walks around with music constantly playing into their earphones, rendering them awkward to communicate with? What about a person who is physically present at some social gathering, but engrossed in sending texts or checking Facebook or Twitter on their phone?

> ***Psychologists who study empathy and compassion are finding that unlike our almost instantaneous responses to physical pain, it takes time for the brain to comprehend the psychological and moral dimensions of a situation. The more distracted we become, and the more emphasis we place on speed at the expense of depth, the less likely and able we are to care (Safran Foer, 2013).***

Make no mistake about it, the technology of emotional withdrawal has become a major industry - and "avoidance sells".

To varying extents, each of us also has the ability to dissociate; that is, to be "non-present" in a moment in time. If you have ever sat and daydreamed, then you have experienced at least the shallow end of dissociation. When you daydream, the environment which you are experiencing is not the environment that is in the room. Someone might even remark, "John, you look like you're a thousand miles away. What are you thinking about?"

If you drive the same stretch of road quite often, you may also have had the similar experience of having absolutely no memory of driving through a large part of it. You remember setting out on your journey, and you can see you have arrived at your destination, but it seems like you must have been driving automatically. This common experience is also somewhere along the shallow end of the scale of dissociative experiences.

For some of us, dissociation can be a little deeper, and may involve repressed memories, blackouts, or even an experience of feeling like we are outside of our body looking on at what is happening to us.

At the very deep end of the scale, some people suffer from dissociative identity disorder (formerly known as Multiple Personality Disorder). This is a condition where a person's mind fragments into different and distinct personalities; each having different names, roles, voices, and often even distinct handwriting.

Since there is such a strong correlation between this disorder and experiences of intense childhood trauma, there is strong support for the theory that it is actually an ingenious tool, which the brain has used to protect a very young person from overwhelming experiences involving great terror and confusion.

In this way, it's almost like a monumental processing task is able to be split up and shared amongst the various personalities (or "alters") so that the "host" personality can feel a greater measure of security. Consciousness of the other characters' experiences occurs only on a "need-to-know" basis.

To varying extents, each one of us also has the ability to dissociate; that is, to be "non-present" in a moment in time

For most of us, dissociating from our painful emotions is not something we are as gifted at, and it is likely that we will need to search for a contractor to do our dissociating for us.

One of the greatest and most popular contractors for dissociation is alcohol. It not only tends to numb physical and emotional pain, but can also have some useful memory-erasing properties.

When I first sat down with Josh (the quiet computer geek on the grievous bodily harm charge), I was struck by the awkwardness of our interaction. He wasn't just shy; he was very shy.

In fact, I found myself instantly recruited into his shyness, and could see straight away how it must be tremendously difficult for him to interact socially without first dulling his anxieties with a drink or three.

For some who contract their dissociation out to alcohol, the flight tool is used to retreat from memories which are too painful to sit with. For others, it may be used to avoid difficult discussions, or even to take the edge off the confronting intimacy of sex.

Whether your chosen dissociation contractor is alcohol, drugs, gaming or something else, it is possible that the feeling or situation which you are medicating for first came into your life during an age when a flight response was the most appropriate response.

4.
THE COST OF FEELING NORMAL

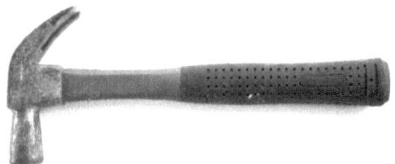

There once was an old man who lived in a rented split-level house, which had a sunken lounge room just a two-inch step down from the dining room.

The old man loved collecting antique furniture and every weekend he would go browsing and shopping at one of the numerous old-wares stores in his village. One weekend, the man found a stunning antique table made of Tasmanian oak, with beautiful turned legs. The table was a large family table, and it was not until he had paid for it and had it delivered that he realised just how long it actually was.

He soon discovered that the table was so long it was not possible for it to fit in either the dining room or the lounge room. The legs would need to span both rooms. Unfortunately, due to the sunken floor, this would mean that the legs would be two inches higher on one side than on the other, but this seemed a small price to pay for the table he had now fallen in love with.

Over the coming weeks, the man would discover that the slope of the table was a little inconvenient. On a few occasions, if he was writing a letter or doing a crossword, pencils would keep rolling down onto the floor. Similarly, oranges would often roll out of his fruit bowl of their own accord. On one occasion a glass of milk actually slid down the table and spilt all over his trousers and the carpet below.

The old man was filled with anger, and he stormed out to his workshed, returning with a saw in his hand. He then began sawing down the legs on the high side of the table, so that it could be forever level, and cease causing him problems.

Since the old man had immediately covered the table with a tablecloth, he never gave the sawn legs another thought, but merely went about his daily business. On the other hand, dinner guests who had never seen the table would occasionally pretend to drop their cutlery, just to take a look at how it was able to cope so well with his flooring.

Seven whole years would pass before the old man's landlord would inform him of the sad news that his rented house was to be sold and that he would need to find another one. The old man did not know where he would live next, but he did know one thing: he would be taking his beloved antique table with him.

With even your limited knowledge of the old man, I wonder whether you know what kind of house he went out looking for?

We all know that the old man would be looking for a split-level house, because there is something very familiar about his predicament. This is the way in which each of us is programmed to think.

Like the old man, each of us has grown up in a home which was in some ways dysfunctional and not entirely straight and level. Similarly, each of us has had to find our own way to cope with our dysfunctional families and to survive in them by using whatever tools we could find to do that and feel normal. As children we must adjust ourselves to fit around the family's dysfunctional elements.

Like the old man, we then get on with our lives as though these adjustments were normal and as though our families were also normal.

Since we have lived in our adjusted and sawn-off state for so long, by the time we are adults we will feel more comfortable and normal in crooked relationships that fit around our brokenness than we will with people and relationships that may be more balanced and healthy.

This is why some people seem to keep finding themselves in the same kinds of unhealthy relationships time after time after time. To people who have come from dysfunctional families (and that's most of us), truly "normal" relationships can actually feel quite uncomfortable.

In some cases, even dangerous relationships (because they feel more familiar to us) might be a lot more comfortable than the uncharted waters of normalcy.

What continues to amaze me is the way in which we are innately attracted to people whose brokenness fits neatly around our own.

In fact, this is almost always the story of our marriages, and unfortunately very often the story of separations and divorces.

We go out into the world with our own particular sawn-off edges and find someone wonderful who "finally fits us." Just like in that sickening movie, we say something cheesy like, "You complete me," when we really mean, "You don't require my screwed-up bits to change too much."

The person who can't say "no" finds and falls in love with the partner who can't hear "no."

The person who needs to rescue other people in order to boost their sense of significance finds a beautiful but hopeless damsel in distress who needs to be rescued regularly.

The person who doesn't want to listen finds a great partner who doesn't want to talk, while the person who hates taking responsibility for their decisions finds someone who never gives them the freedom to make any.

Isn't love grand? And don't we really love not having to adjust too much to fit someone?

If the families we grew up in are responsible for our understanding of what "normal" might look like, it's frightening to think that, in looking for a partner, we are to some extent looking for a coalition of agreement; someone to agree with our "normal" and to make us feel even more right than we did before.

For instance, I've seen more than my share of couples who have unconsciously agreed to keep their marriage relationally shallow. Other couples agree that conflict should be loud, abusive and reactive. In fact, it's amazing what two people in love will reinforce in each other.

When David and Sarah came to see me for counselling, they had discovered a book on "domestic discipline" in which the wife was required to confess anything she had done wrong during the day, so that the husband could put her over his knee and spank her for each of her daily crimes.

Thankfully I had been counselling for long enough to know that other people are no more weird than you or I; their stories just make sense in different ways.

Therefore my burning question - as with most couples - was this: what is it about their respective stories which makes this seem so normal for them? If you're prepared to sit and listen for long enough, there is always a great answer to that question (just as there was in

David and Sarah's case).

The answer will also make sense of why they found each other and ended up together.

In fact, our occupations and careers also have a funny way of choosing us because of the particular tools we had to pick up to fit our families.

As we discovered earlier, there are some people who have had traumatic experiences in childhood where they needed to dissociate from reality in order to cope with overwhelming or confusing events. People with this highly developed ability tend to end up in careers where a superhuman ability to dissociate is a great benefit. Although they may struggle to find and maintain depth in their relationships, they make excellent police, paramedics or military servicepeople.

Similarly, people who have grown up in families where they learned to be responsible for others and to rescue them will find themselves drawn to nursing, counselling and other caring professions.

People whose lives have taught them about the paramount importance of being in control of others might be drawn to teaching or management, or they may find themselves employed as prison wardens or directors of nursing.

It would be cynical to suggest that we are only drawn to these and other careers by the damage we have suffered. On the contrary, I am suggesting that our childhood adaptations create for us certain abilities which others will find useful and profitable, just as we have also done.

Whilst it is important for us to recognise the particular strengths our stories have built into us, it is even more important to be wary of the profound self-deceit they can instil in us.

For many of us, the realisation that our families were not perfect, healthy or "normal" all of the time will be too uncomfortable to accept. Since the foundations of our whole sense of security are built on our family during those early years, it is likely that we will go to great lengths to protect the normalcy of our story.

To accept that our parents might have made mistakes that caused us damage seems like a dishonouring and ungrateful exercise. Similarly, to accept that we were abused, neglected or traumatised by anyone at all is a confronting realisation. These situations can tempt us to prefer to reframe "normal" in the present in order to make the abnormal past more bearable to carry.

> *For many of us, the realisation that our families were not perfect, healthy or "normal" all of the time will be too uncomfortable to accept*

For example, although only a small number of those who have suffered childhood sexual abuse will go on to become sex offenders, paedophiles do tend to have some overwhelmingly similar histories of childhood sexual abuse, which they have normalised and integrated into their own sexuality.

Are their desires normal? They might tell you that they are. Once we go on to hear the whole story of their lives, we will also be forced to concede that it is at least "normal" for them and for the story from which they have emerged. Perhaps it has also been easier for them to integrate this perverted experience than to process the devastating disempowerment they have faced at the hands of another.

In fact, all sexual deviances tend to have this in common: a fusion of the person's orientation with the circumstances of their early sexual experiences (or observed sexual experiences).

I wonder if you can remember the very first time you became aware of using your dysfunctional tools.

When people are asked this question, they almost always reply too quickly with a "no." But this is a question which each of us needs to sit with. It's a question worthy of our full attention, since the answer will be very helpful in the case of any tool you hope to replace.

The first answer which comes into your head will probably seem too trivial and irrelevant, but go with it anyway. Even if the memory snapshot which comes to you is probably not the very first time you picked up a particular tool, it will be no less helpful if it is at least your first conscious memory of using it (or seeing someone else use it).

To make the most of this book, take the time to record these memories of early use in the response panel over the page. Was your first recollection of using your dysfunctional tool a response to something?

Was it a flight, fight or freeze response? Was it a tool handed down to you, or which you observed working for somebody else? Was it a means for you to feel normal in what was an abnormal situation? Is it a thought or behaviour around which you have formed a coalition with somebody else? Is it something which your chosen occupation or career has positively reinforced?

The answers to these questions will be incredibly helpful in the task of identifying why you first took up and adopted your blunt and broken tools. This can provide some of the best clues as to what you might want these tools to do for you now.

NAME THE TOOL:

RETROSPECTIVE

WHAT IS YOUR FIRST MEMORY OF EVER PICKING UP THIS TOOL?

5.
WHAT ARE YOU LOOKING FOR?

When people realise that they have been wielding blunt and broken tools for most of their lives, at an incredible cost to themselves and those they love, it's natural for them to want to beat themselves up a little. It's also easy for them to begin to think of themselves as stupid or even a bit hopeless.

Sometimes this kind of self-assessment can cause people to just give up trying and resign themselves to the fact that they will probably always do what they have always done.

To define ourselves as stupid is to forget the fact that it was probably not our adult selves who picked up the tools in the first place. As we have seen, many of our dysfunctional tools are picked up during childhood, and often people don't sit and consider them with an adult's thinking for very long at all.

So if we must be negative about our adoption of dysfunctional tools, we should at least be accurate and consider them to be childish rather than foolish. When our time for beating ourselves up is over though, we will find it a lot more empowering if we are able to stop and celebrate our incredible resourcefulness and creativity.

We did, after all, find tools which worked to some extent to produce some kind of positive result (possibly our very survival). We know this to be true since, without some kind of payoff, we would have abandoned our dysfunctional tools a long time ago.

Since most of our blunt and broken tools cause us shame or embarrassment, it will take us way out of our comfort zone to begin seeing them as something positive; but positive they are.

Since we are too lazy and too clever to use something which is only causing us inconvenience, you can be sure that we are only using these tools because they are giving us something we feel we need.

I once heard a great counsellor say to a client, "Whenever you are being manipulated by someone you should always ask yourself, 'what is it that I need so much from this person that I'm prepared to let them manipulate me?'"

Sit with that thought for a moment, because if you miss it you will miss a key truth which is crucial to you moving forward.

Whether you're conscious of it or not, the needs which drive you to keep picking up your dysfunctional tools are so great and pressing that you have internally convinced yourself they are worth all of the costs. If it were not so, you would have had no problem putting your tools down by now. That's why hating your tools a little more does very little to empower you to be free from them. You're too intelligent to use something which is not helping you in some way, even though denial may be giving you a great big fight.

To accept that you have deep needs and dependencies is a difficult thing to do. It's a lot easier to convince yourself that you are silly or hopeless for continuing to do the things you hate, since that takes the pressure of having to change off you. Accepting deep inner weakness takes a special kind of courage, but without it you cannot go forward.

We are too lazy and too clever to use something which is only causing us inconvenience

So what is it about your blunt, broken tool that you appreciate? (Does this question make you uncomfortable?) What is it doing for you? How is it serving you? As we have seen in the previous chapter, the story of when you first picked it up can be a wonderful clue as to why you continue to do it again and again.

John had a long list of problems resulting from his pornography habit. He did not need to hate his addiction any more than he did, even though hating it had been at least enough to make him present for counselling. John needed to discover what was driving him. What was so enticing that he was prepared to let it cost him so much?

John's first recollection of encountering pornography was at the age of thirteen. His younger brothers were using it, and he felt a little left out. When other boys were using pornography at school, and talking about it all the time, he felt even more of a drive to be the same as others. Unlike many cultures around the world, our Western culture does not offer young men any single defining moment of initiation into manhood. There is no point at which men say, "You're one of us now," and so it is not uncommon for men of all ages to reach for something that allays these kinds of anxieties.

John discovered that pornography was especially a problem for him when he felt lonely or disconnected. He craved appropriate physical touch and more intimacy and emotional depth in his relationships.

Since pornography's subjects appeared to always be offering themselves eagerly with the lure of a kind of intimacy, this type of fantasy was especially hard to resist. Like a thirsty man who has found saltwater, John would drink deeply and desperately, but receive only more feelings of shame and isolation as a result. Our broken tools can be cruel like that.

There are no formulae for diagnosing exactly what attracts you to your dysfunctional tools. Since you are a special and unique individual, your story will be unique too, and will have shaped your own particular thirsts, longings, desires and weaknesses.

Whilst probably few of us will ever struggle in exactly the same way, or for exactly the same reasons, there is a certain familiarity to the key themes of our struggles. See if you can identify with any of these broad categories of deep desires:

SECURITY

Imagine for a moment that you are caught in an earthquake. The walls are shaking, the floor is shaking; you run outside and the ground beneath your feet is shaking more violently than you ever thought it could. You long to find just one solid object which will remain still, and which you could hold onto with all of your might. For some people, this is the story of their daily existence.

If you have ever had events in your life unexpectedly shake the whole earth from under you, then it's likely that you find it very difficult to feel safe and secure. Tina was one lady who had grown up in a very dysfunctional family, in which she had been repeatedly raped by her older brother over several years. Her mother was harsh and verbally abusive, and the rest of family life was filled with violence and alcoholism. The pornography which contributed to her brother's attacks was not considered a problem, so its presence in the family home left her constantly on edge.

With such a high level of insecurity in her world, there was always a good chance that Tina would be attracted to a man with enough of the familiar traits of her family that she would not feel totally unsettled. Her husband is a good man, but yes, has a short temper. He also is a man who uses sex as his medication for stress; an especially unfortunate trait for one married to a sexual abuse victim, but very common.

When our world is shaking with deep insecurity, we reach for what we know and for something solid or constant. It's no wonder people suffering from obsessive-compulsive disorder reach for dozens of small things in their world that they can micro-manage. It's no wonder that the person with an eating disorder obsesses about her weight, and finds extreme ways to be in control of it. It's also no surprise that the overwhelmed teenager is self-harming, or that the traumatised asylum-seeker is now abusing his wife and family.

When our world is out of control, the sense that we can have a little control over at least something is a great comfort. It's amazing what great lengths we will go to in order to find that solid, grounding reassurance.

RESPECT

People need to know that other people take them seriously. Sociologist Hugh Mackay describes this as the strongest of the deep desires which "makes us tick" (Mackay, 2010, x) This could be the reason why the Western world has become so litigious. Do Westerners sue because they really need to or because they have not been taken seriously and must really insist upon it?

"I'll teach those arrogant jerks that they've messed with the wrong guy!"

Could this also be the reason why people get so worked up in chatrooms, on social media, or behind the wheel of their car?

When husbands and wives neglect to take each other seriously, devastatingly stupid decisions are made in marriages. It would be interesting to know what high percentage of extra-marital affairs have merely been a response to feeling taken for granted.

"There are plenty of other people out there who will take me seriously if you won't!"

Ashley Madison is an online dating site specifically targeting married people who are planning on cheating. According to their own research, there is always a huge spike in memberships on the Monday after Mother's Day. The website's founder, Noel Biderman, provided his best theory for this statistical upturn:

"On Mother's Day, women in general expect to be celebrated by their partners. However, for many already suffering from a lack of appreciation, this day represents a continuation of neglect and disappointment" (Houston, 2012).

IDENTITY

It's very important to be able to tell yourself who you are, but also to be happy and comfortable about it when you do. If you stop and listen to how you introduce yourself to others, what usually comes next after you say your name?

If you are like most of us, you will go on to identify yourself in terms of what you do. You might say, "I'm an accountant" or "I'm a mum." You might even define yourself by your marital status, or by something you are passionate about: "I'm an antiwhaling activist."

But who do you tell yourself you are? And when you're pushed to tell others who you are, do you find that you tell them the truth? Are you proud or ashamed of the truth about who you are? It seems that being comfortable in your own skin is a rare quality these days.

Certainly there are times in our lives when our sense of identity is more difficult to find and feel comfortable with than other times. For many of us, adolescence is the first challenging time for being comfortable with who we are. There are so many options and big life-changing decisions which young people have to make during this time. Ironically, this is at a time in which they may feel very strong pressure from friends and family to meet their expectations too.

Adolescence is also a time in which even our physical body is in a state of development and often unwanted change, so it's easy to feel quite disappointed with who we are on both sides of our skin.

Identity is a difficult issue in the stages of life when we are not positioned where we would like to be.

Perhaps we are single when we would like to have been married a long time ago. Perhaps we are divorced, and the choice to remain married was not within our control; we were abandoned or rejected. Maybe we are currently without work, and have been unemployed for so long that it has become deeply embarrassing for us. Maybe we have even come to question whether we are employable at all. Are we a contributor to society, or likely to forever be a burden upon it?

If we do not have a consistent and strong sense of identity, all kinds of life circumstances are liable to send us into a tailspin.

Identity issues which have been lying dormant in the background can also rear their ugly heads suddenly. People used to talk about turning 40 and going through some kind of midlife crisis. In these days of great change, when people may have three different careers each lasting about 20 years, an identity crisis can happen at any significant age. Commonly people turning 30 will find that this milestone presents such a moment of self-evaluation and reckoning that it plunges them into deep despair. School reunions are also a difficult time for most of us as we are brought once again to face some of our early formative identity consultants, and wonder whether they will approve of who we have become.

It's very important to be able to tell yourself who you are, but also to be happy and comfortable about it when you do

So who do you think you are? Because who you think you are is everything. You are, after all, the world's premier expert on the subject of you. If you have a poor sense of identity, it's very likely that you will already have reached for some imperfect tools to build a false identity around. It hurts to dislike who you are, so it's also likely that you will have picked up a few coping tools to medicate the pain.

INTIMACY

This is the deep desire for the mutuality of being able to know somebody and be fully known by them. It is a deeply fulfilling human state when we are connected to another person in ways that go beyond the superficial, right down to the very depths of our hearts. Intimacy requires of us that we get beyond the terror of having our naked soul exposed, all for the chance to be loved - failings and all - right down to our roots.

To experience intimacy requires great personal vulnerability and risk, but is perhaps the most authentic of all of our human adventures. In fact, it is the true adventure which many of us long for without realising it.

Since we are born for the adventure of true intimacy, it should not be surprising that those who do not find it will always be vulnerable to finding lesser, counterfeit adventures. For some, it may be the thrill of flirting and the challenge of attracting the attention and desire of the opposite sex. For others, it may be the bottomless underworld of internet pornography or lewd online chatrooms. For many, it will be the quest for the next rush of adrenaline on some BASE jump or envelope-pushing Alpine summit.

Since I am a rock climbing enthusiast in my other life, I am often asked what attracts me to the fear and adrenaline of the sport. To be honest, that's actually the aspect of the sport I don't enjoy. The attraction for me is the beautiful rugged places that rock climbing takes me, and the challenge of making a bare natural feature of rock totally safe to fall from at any point. Call me a coward, but the fear and adrenaline are an unpleasant reality which I occasionally have to endure to partake in the sport I enjoy. However, rock climbing does create plenty of opportunities to rub shoulders with some seriously hardcore adrenaline junkies.

At the extreme end of the spectrum are "soloists" who climb without ropes and continue to push their limits through tougher and tougher climbs.

Interestingly, they don't tend to die climbing, but often in another adventure sport for which they are less prepared; one which most of us would not be led into by the addictive allure of adrenaline. There is also a fairly reliable profile for the solo climber. I have never met a person who didn't climb the way they live - and the soloist is no exception. They are people who are quite difficult to engage on any deep kind of level, oblivious to the loved ones who they seem destined to leave behind at some point.

To experience intimacy requires great personal vulnerability and risk, but is perhaps the most authentic of all of our human adventures

Before we stop to criticise them or pass judgement, we should keep in mind that the soloist or the adrenaline junkie represent only a very small percentage of those who have fallen prey to a life-controlling counterfeit adventure. We were all born for the rush and teetering feeling of vulnerability which intimacy calls us towards. If we don't find it in relationships of depth, we will surely quench our thirst for it elsewhere.

BELONGING

We all need a place to belong and a tribe to call our own. For Tara it was a struggle to find exactly where that place of belonging was. Growing up in a family where domestic violence was severe and frequent, she always felt a sense of alienation from her family, somewhat like a visitor from another planet.

To compensate for the chaos at home, Tara threw herself into her school work and soon became both a straight-A student and a star of the athletics track. School was more than a second home - it was a place of refuge and a place to belong.

Through the difficult teenage years Tara would discover that not all of the girls were thrilled about sharing their social circle with a good-looking high achiever. When nasty and baseless rumours began to circulate about her, Tara quickly found herself without a place to belong. Despairing to the point of suicide, she desperately called out to God. When she embarked on a new life as a born-again Christian, she found herself entering into a new and supportive community. Church was a positive place to belong, and a home in which she was affirmed, encouraged and nurtured.

We all need a community which embraces us, feels similar to us in some way and affirms some part of us. Perhaps the most fundamental experience of a "place to belong" for most of us will be our own family. Without this kind of basic foundation in a stable and happy place of belonging, people are prone to finding all kinds of means of fulfilling a deep unmet desire. If they don't find a sporting team to belong to and be fanatical about, then it may be a motorcycle gang, a drug culture or some other social subculture. The need to belong somewhere runs deep in our veins.

Somewhere in the intersection of our two great needs for a sense of identity and a sense of belonging is our deep need to belong and find acceptance from those of our own gender. Author John

Eldridge (2001, pp61-62) suggests that it is the deep and burning question within every man's heart: "Have I got what it takes to be a man?" For women, the desire to be embraced by their own is equally compelling. It is this strong desire to feel affirmed in our masculinity which drives men to do all kinds of stupid things to prove by external means that we "belong."

Unfortunately some of the silly bravado and chest-beating intended to prove masculinity can alienate other men. Michael was one such man whose outward expressions of traditional masculinity were not as pronounced as those of his older brother, so that his father was unsure how to relate to him. Michael began to ask deep burning questions of himself like, "I wonder if I am gay?" Just like many alpha males, Michael was forming an identity around superficial external expressions of sexuality which provided a shortcut to a sense of belonging with a group of people who were on a common journey.

> *We all need a community which embraces us, feels similar to us in some way and affirms some part of us*

For Michael the gay scene was more than a community with shared interests. It was a place to belong. These days Michael will tell you that his gay identity was the broken tool he used to numb the pain of being rejected by his father and to gain a sense of belonging with others on a similar journey. Whilst that's certainly not the story of every person who identifies as gay, Michael's story is not uncommon.

SIGNIFICANCE

Ask anyone what they would like to do if they could do anything with their life and you will find that almost all of us have this one thing in common: we all want to do something significant and enduring, to leave a legacy and to make a lasting difference.

However, the all-important question is not whether we want to be significant, but whether we need to be significant.

For some, the unfulfilled deep desire to be someone can become an all-consuming and life-controlling drive.

Jason was a man on a mission to be someone famous and important. Within his heart was a deep thirst to be a hero to many, and he had several options as to how he might achieve this goal. Although he would admit that his need to rescue people on a significant scale was more about him than those he might rescue, his self-awareness was not deep enough to overcome it.

This powerful desire was also playing havoc with his relationships and his no-nonsense fiancée was not willing to begin a career as sidekick to a superhero. If this superhero had a name it would probably have been "anti-dad," since Jason's drive was largely based on a strong contempt for his complacent and low-achieving father.

We would all like to know that we are at least a bit significant, but how exactly do we measure significance? One of the problems is that it is difficult to quantify and assess.

Perhaps the biggest counterfeit measure of significance, which people turn to in many cultures, is wealth. If we could put a dollars and cents measure on it, perhaps this would be a concrete way to prove our significance and compare it with the significance of those around us. If our house, our car and our toys are the envy of the neighbourhood, this might prove we are significant to the society which has fittingly rewarded us for our most valuable contribution.

For internet gamers like Ronny, a surrogate sense of his online character's significance is enough to feed a life-controlling habit. While the online army he commands may not exist in the real world, his community of flesh and blood admirers certainly does.

Should he tuck his baby into bed tonight? Should he go to bed with his wife, who tries in vain to seduce him night after night? How are these things even possible for someone like Ronny when he knows that so many people are counting on him to turn up in cyberspace and lead them into battle?

If you find his story despicable or impossible to relate to, then stop for a moment and consider this: how is Ronny any different to the workaholic who is selling out his family to climb the corporate ladder? How is he any different to the woman who feels taken for granted by her husband and has begun flirting with a young stud at the gym who seems to have taken an interest in her?

Go into your nearest city and you will see initials tagged high up on railway bridges, buildings and billboards by young people who risked their lives for a moment of significance. Many people each year pay hundreds of thousands of dollars to climb Mt Everest or K2, despite the atrocious rate of fatalities.

Open the Guinness Book of Records and ponder the multitude of contrived feats by which all kinds of people have claimed their own little slice of significance.

Above all, it is important to consider your own pursuits, dreams and life goals in light of this deep desire for significance. You may be surprised by what you learn.

ACCEPTANCE

Within the hearts of all of us is a deep desire to know that we are okay and that others accept us for who and what we are. You will recall from chapter one that shame is the voice which tells us the opposite: that we are far from okay, and something is clearly wrong with us.

Shame can be difficult to argue with because no matter how kind other people may be to us, we alone know the truth of our darkest thoughts, words and behaviours. It's no wonder many of us believe we are not worthy of anyone else's acceptance, and yet we still look for it.

Laura found it especially hard to believe that anyone could find her worthy. Her childhood was a case of the most miserable and shocking abuse and neglect. She had spent the vast majority of her adulthood in prison, and the rest trying to avoid it. When I met her for the first time, she smiled as she reported that she had now been out of prison for the longest period of her adult life: two and a half years.

As she told me of her life and her current goals, I could see that Laura was a very good person underneath, with a great loyalty to those she cared for and a big heart to serve others. When I began describing the good qualities I saw in her, she was lost for words and tears came to her eyes. Having someone affirm and appreciate her was like a sunshower in the midst of a dry and parched desert. Here was a lady who just longed to be loved and accepted.

Like so many people, Laura had a love/hate relationship with people who grew close to her. She wanted to have people close to her but greatly feared having them close enough to hurt her.

Her fear of rejection was so overwhelming it caused her to put people at a distance by lashing out violently, which was why her life had been punctuated by prison terms.

Many people, like Laura, are so crippled by their fear of rejection that they avoid any arena which might bring them a sense of acceptance. Life is a risk and relationships are an adventure, but for those who have suffered deep rejection, the challenge can feel like Mt Everest.

So what are you looking for?

When we view our own blunt and broken tools in an effort to

understand them, we must consider our own deep needs from two different points of view. That's because we will likely discover that we are using some of our broken tools in order to fulfil our basic needs, and using others in response to the flip-side of those needs.

Laura's story demonstrates that it is not just our need for acceptance which motivates us, but also the fear of rejection, which is its ugly flip-side.

While we crave intimacy, we also have to come to terms with its ugly twin: fear of being trapped, smothered or stuck with connections that we don't want; that make us feel out of our depth.

We need security and a sense of control over our world, but we must also deal with the fact that absolute empowerment leaves us open to absolute blame when things go pear-shaped.

Similarly, not only do we need to discover and be grounded in our true sense of identity, but we must also face potential disgust over some aspects of who that will lead us to discover. We yearn for the respect of others - to have them take us seriously and validate our contribution as significant - but we fear that we may then have a long way to fall if we ever gain it. We would love to have a sense of belonging to a group like ourselves, which embraces us as one of its own, but we rightly fear the resulting alienation from those outside of the tribe, and perhaps even the resulting ridicule, persecution or conflicts.

There is a powerful reason why you continue to take up your own particular dysfunctional tools. If you did not pick them up in response to one of the deep human needs which we have discussed in this chapter, then the tools may have been handed to you via close observation of somebody else using them; or they may have been taken up instinctively in a moment of urgency and then become a lifelong pattern. In most cases it will be a combination of two or three of these factors.

You need to stop for a moment, and take the time and courage to look deeply into the question of what your dysfunctional tools are doing for you. Until you find some genuine answers, there is little point in moving on to the next chapter.

Be sure to take the time once again to reflect on what you are learning about your dysfunctional tools. Use the response panel on the last page of this chapter to list any of the motivations which are becoming clearer to you as you sit with the question, "What am I looking for?"

As with all healing, you are probably not likely to find a breakthrough in a vacuum or on a desert island

As with all healing, you are probably not likely to find a breakthrough in a vacuum or on a desert island. "As iron sharpens iron, so one person sharpens the wits of another" (Proverbs 27:17, GW). Whether through a good friend, a counsellor, a partner, a church or a support group, you will only gain this deep understanding of yourself in true community.

Like a man who buys a dishwasher and stubbornly refuses to connect it to the tap and to a power point, you can try to fight against your basic design specifications, but healing just doesn't work that way. Just like brokenness, healing is going to involve other people.

NAME THE TOOL:

POSITIVE

IN WHAT WAYS IS THIS TOOL DOING SOMETHING FOR YOU?

6.
ENGAGING THE ALTERNATIVE

By now you are aware of the different dysfunctional tools which you continue to use. You have counted the cost of using them, and know that the cost is unsustainable and unacceptable. You have also considered the first time you remember using your blunt and broken tools, and this may have given you a strong insight into what you are continuing to use them for.

You should therefore be able to answer the question which was put to you in the last chapter: "What are you looking for?" It is only when you can consistently answer this question that you will have any idea why you need to pick up any tool at all to meet your needs.

When you replace your old tools with better tools, like Dr Payne you will never return to the inconvenience and high personal cost of the old tools. You will be pleased to know that it is finally time to replace your old dysfunctional tools, and it all begins with three simple questions.

LESSONS FROM BUYING A MOBILE PHONE

There would be few people in the Western world who have not yet had the experience of buying a mobile phone or paying one off for far too long on some dodgy contract. You might agree that with the incredible variety of handsets on offer and fierce competition between manufacturers, choosing a phone can be a daunting decision.

Since I was a relatively late convert to smartphones, I found myself making a decision in the midst of what seemed like a brand war. Within my circle of friends and colleagues, two distinct groups emerged and both were equally passionate about their respective choice of brand. To ask for advice from friends of either group was more than personal; it was like stepping into a civil war. How could I ever hope to receive objective advice, when for some of my friends this issue drilled deep down to their sense of belonging? It was going to be tough.

Before too long I realised that fans of the particular major brands were largely divided along the lines of function. Each respective group represented distinct needs and priorities in terms of what they needed this pocket computer to do. For a small number of people it was actually about making phone calls. For some, it was about email and reliable web access - the tools of business. For others, it was all about multimedia and the ability to play music, take great photos and upload them easily to social media sites.

I soon realised that the best question was not, "Which brand should I get?" since it would be a relatively easy choice once I knew what I needed my smartphone to do. Once my own priorities and needs were clear, the best question I could ask was:

"What do others use to meet the needs I am trying to satisfy?"

When it comes to replacing your own bent and broken tools, this question is perhaps one of the most important. Rather than reinventing the wheel, what are other people doing to find security, significance, belonging, identity, or whatever it is that you are looking for? What tools do other people use to cope when their situations feel unbearable? You can use the response panel at the end of this chapter to begin to record your thoughts.

LESSONS FROM CHOOSING A UNIVERSITY

A number of years ago, when I was contemplating further studies in counselling, I began to survey the large range of universities which were offering my chosen qualification. It was decision time, and I could see no clear-cut formula for weighing up the different options.

In my confusion, I remembered some advice which my boss had once shared with me: "The best way to see what an institution is like is to see who is at the top, and what kinds of people the institution turns out." That advice makes a lot of practical sense.

By knowing the DNA of the institution's leader, I gain a reliable understanding of the culture which is likely to flow on to all levels of the organisation. By seeing what kinds of people the institution turns out, I gain a reliable insight into the kind of person it is going to shape me to be. Are they people who I respect? Do they gain employment? What reputations do they have in their respective industries? These kinds of questions practically made my decision for me. Almost everybody who I looked up to in the counselling field had come through the one local institution. What a powerful thing one piece of good advice can be.

It turns out that my boss's clever advice is also some of the best advice that I can give you for replacing your blunt and broken tools:

"Who do I really want to be like, and what do people I really respect use to achieve their results?"

Use the response panel at the end of the chapter to record your thoughts once again.

BORROWING TOOLS FROM MY NEIGHBOUR

When it comes to using real tools from a real toolbox I'm more of a part-time plonker than a handyman. That's why my own toolbox is a simple one with only a few generic "must-have" tools.

My neighbour Rodrigo, on the other hand, is a true weekend warrior. To be honest, I'm not even sure if he actually has a toolbox at all; what he has is a well-equipped workroom with functional workbenches, fitted power tools and well-organised shelves and tool-hooks. It's a very impressive workshop, from which the sounds of fruitful labour and song often emanate.

Since Rodrigo is such a good neighbour, and we frequently talk across the fence or in each other's houses, he has offered to lend me his tools whenever I need them. He has even helped me with a few handyman projects (or rather, I have ended up helping him). Like most men, I find that asking is the hardest part; admitting that somebody else has the tool I need, and being humble enough to say so.

Perhaps that's why at times when my life has been out of control and on the brink of ruin I have found it so hard to confide in someone else or to seek professional help. As a counsellor I have often reflected that persuading men to attend counselling is like trying to convince a cat to take a bath.

When it comes to replacing our blunt and broken tools, there are sure to be other people in our world with far better tools than ours. Are we prepared to humble ourselves enough to admit our need? To look around our circle of friends or go further in an effort to find a professional who could coach us or introduce us to a whole new toolbox? The third big question which we should ask when attempting to replace our blunt and broken tools is this one:

"Who could I ask to help me learn to use better tools?"

Take the time to sit with this question and then record your thoughts in the response panel at the end of the chapter.

CHALLENGING YOUR OLD THINKING

Sometimes replacing a dysfunctional tool begins by disputing a hardwired thought process with some new and positive self-talk.

Cindy was a woman who had never truly emerged as a differentiated adult, but had remained a compliant daughter for almost 50 years. Since she had never been able to stand up to her father or express the slightest rebellion as a teenager, she had grown resentful of the life which she felt others had chosen for her. When these feelings came to a head, Cindy was already a long-time wife and mother of two, but would tell you that she never really chose the man she was with. Instead, she felt that she had been pressured into marrying him by her parents. It was true that her father was a stubborn and unreasonable old man whom everyone else in the family feared, pandered to, and stepped carefully around.

Standing up to her father was still unthinkable, so instead she began expressing her suppressed teenage rebellion towards her husband, in the form of unfaithfulness and accusations that he was trying to control her.

In therapy, I told Cindy the story of how my daily commute to work involved turning right across two busy lanes of oncoming traffic. Although the turn was a legal turn, not everybody was happy about it all of the time. Drivers in the right lane were often forced to bank up behind me for a little while as I waited for a break in the traffic, and many of them were quite impatient about it. On some days drivers behind me would honk their horns or do a big wheel spin as they angrily pulled out from behind me. On other days drivers would raise a finger or two or yell something out of their window.

Even though this did not happen most days, the unpleasant days were enough to make me change my route to work and take a long and contrived detour, which did not involve the dreaded right-hand turn.

After many detours and much personal inconvenience, one day I came to my senses and realised that the right-hand turn I needed to make was neither illegal nor unreasonable. Some people were just being impatient and rude, and I was allowing it to become my problem, just like Cindy and her obstinate old Dad. I recounted to Cindy that what had set me free from the oppression of those impatient drivers was to simply decide not to take their feelings upon myself as my responsibility, and to say to myself, "It's only a right-hand turn."

For Cindy, the thought that other people's strong feelings should not motivate her into action was almost crazy. I will never forget her reaction when I suggested, for instance, that she could talk to her father about the way he speaks to her and let him know that she's not okay with it. Clearly the very thought was giving her palpitations, and a look of horror fell upon her, like I had just asked her to jump out of a speeding train. "It's only a right-hand turn," I said.

Sometimes replacing a dysfunctional tool begins by disputing a hardwired thought process with some new and positive self-talk.

To Cindy's credit, she took the opportunity to do what was absolutely taboo in her family: she dared to address the way her father spoke to her and to her children. She recounted with a smile how, in that moment of sheer terror as she stepped out upon the relational precipice, she had had to steel herself, and to say internally, "It's only a right-hand turn."

For Cindy, this small turn in her thinking was enough to bring profound change into her life, and into the way that she perceived herself and her responsibilities.

For many of us, retooling our minds will be as simple as replacing old thinking with fresh self-talk and a new positive mantra.

Wal also made a small change in thinking which made a profound difference. His violent and aggressive daughter had increasingly shirked responsibility for her baby son and had high expectations of what Wal and his wife should be doing for her as live-in grandparents. Wal felt that they had become stuck in a no-win situation in which his daughter was never going to take responsibility for herself and her baby, and Wal and his wife were becoming increasingly cornered and controlled by her and her aggressive outbursts.

After Wal's daughter had been out for a big night at the clubs with her friends, picking up and soothing her crying baby the next morning had become his responsibility. This practice had started innocently enough as Wal's attempt to be helpful and make the life of this single mum a bit easier. He was also avoiding any unpleasant confrontations when trying to wake her up. By the time Wal and his wife presented for counselling, this had become almost a daily responsibility for the two of them, regardless of whether their daughter had been out clubbing or not. On the surface of things they were stuck, and had differing opinions on what they should do about it.

After much counselling, it would emerge that Wal had a love/hate relationship with these primary care responsibilities. Compared to the other two adults in the house, he experienced close to three times as much anxiety over the baby being left to cry, and was aware that comforting him was a way of allaying guilt over the way he had raised his own children. Though difficult to admit, it was even a means of replacing them.

He confessed that the close bond he was building with his grandson was the only positive male relationship of his entire life. Although he knew it was preventing the boy's mother from forming a similar strong bond, all he could see was how incredibly painful it would be to step back from the child in any way.

When Wal was eventually able to see this dysfunctional tool for what it was, he could begin addressing all of the personal needs it satisfied. He was not a bad man, but like his grandson, he felt unable to cope with the pain and discomfort of being left all alone. For Wal, this was a discomfort which he needed to endure to fully emerge as a complete adult. For that reason, telling himself that he couldn't do it or that the emotional pain was impossible for him to bear would have been unhelpful. I challenged Wal to begin retooling his thinking by telling himself, "Enduring this separateness might be incredibly painful, but it's not impossible."

For many people, embracing the pain and discomfort involved in positive change will begin with simply retooling your stubborn thought process around what is impossible and what you can't do:

"Never smoking again is going to be very hard, but it's not impossible."

"Refusing to eat junk food will be downright tough, but I know I'm tougher."

"Saying 'no' to my partner is going to make things uncomfortable for a while, but who said a healthy relationship should be comfortable all the time?"

"Properly forgiving this person is going to be like walking out into the surf. As the waves of pain and hatred relentlessly crash against me, I will smile and remember that they are making me stronger."

"Ending this is going to hurt me, but not ending it is going to kill me."

THOROUGH AND CONVINCING REPLACEMENT

It's not enough to simply dispute your old excuses, find a better tool which someone else is using successfully, and decide to swap it for your own. You must be thoroughly convinced that your new tools are better tools, and you must have a well thought out plan for exactly how and when you intend to implement them. It's critical that you thoroughly understand what you are using your tools to do for you. If you replace only one of a tool's functions, it may not become redundant - and you are likely to continue picking it up.

You must be fully convinced that any new tool is up to the task. Changing an old habit takes conviction, even if you are replacing it with something good. Although failure is a normal part of progress, persistent failures bring unnecessary discouragement.

It's better to set out with a plan which you believe is going to work than to be plagued with doubts from day one.

A WISE COMPANION

Sometimes thorough and convincing replacement of your dysfunctional tools is going to require a second opinion from somebody with wisdom and insight, whom you can trust with your whole story. For many of us this is very difficult to do for the first time.

A qualified and experienced counsellor, psychologist or therapist can often give you the confidence you need to go further into your healing, since they will hopefully be a stranger, and your relationship with them will only be a contractual one for the purposes of talking about your stuff. Knowing that they are keeping your story in strict confidence will feel a whole lot safer for you as you begin to explore many of its twists and turns for the first time and try to make sense of your blunt and broken tools.

If you find yourself out of your depth and running for cover, a good counsellor will not hunt you down or put a guilt trip on you for not calling them. They will simply be there for you once you feel ready to re-engage.

"But what are therapists actually there to do? What is their purpose?" I am often asked this question by counselling students, and I like to reply with this story:

In 1998, I was backpacking around Europe with my wife, another couple and their trusty Kombi Van, "Enoch." Only another traveller could understand how, after two weeks in Europe, one might become heartily sick of churches, monuments and ancient ruins, and might also become considerably more difficult to impress. By the time we had reached Greece the ancient city of Mycenae had lured us in only with the promise of the oldest surviving monument in Europe: the Lion Gate. On the site of the ancient city's excavation there stood a mysterious doorway, which appeared to be the top of a stone staircase leading down into the earth. There were no signs, no plaques and no explanations for the staircase, and it seemed that it had not caught the attention of any other tourists.

For me, the dark and mysterious staircase was both intriguing and scary. In fact, I had not taken too many steps down into the darkness before I began to look over my shoulder to see if my fellow adventurer Aaron was with me - and thankfully he was.

The air was damp, and the old stone stairs very slippery. Since there was no handrail, and we had no idea where the staircase led, we watched our every step carefully. To further slow our progress into the abyss, every few steps took us further into such deep darkness that we had to stop and let our eyes adjust.

The descent was slow, unsettling, but still strangely alluring. Although I was doing my best to be brave, I knew there was no way in the world I would have walked down there alone. It was only the comfort of Aaron's voice beside me that was keeping me going.

When it seemed the tunnel could scarcely grow any darker, our eyes barely made out the flat wall of a dead-end up ahead. The atmosphere was thick and damp and the confines claustrophobic. At that moment we were suddenly surrounded by a swarm of bats, frantically squeaking and flapping past our faces. Instinctively - and without a word - we turned as one and began a dangerous dash up the slippery stairs, almost outrunning the poor creatures we had unintentionally cornered.

Incredibly, our fifty-metre scramble towards the light brought us to the top with injuries only to our sense of masculinity. Puffing, panting and fright soon gave way to wide smiles and laughter from both of us and our wives, who had witnessed our panic.

What is a therapist and what are they there to do? They are simply there to walk beside us as we go down into dark and scary places which we would never have the courage to explore alone.

Sometimes their voice will motivate and encourage us to keep going. At other times they will need to remind us why we wanted to go there in the first place. Their greatest gift will be to stand bravely beside us when it feels like everything is out of control and desperately frightening. The calmness we draw from a counsellor who has been there before with so many people is a gift you must experience to truly appreciate.

Ideally, the therapist you choose should not be afraid of bats... (Sorry Aaron).

AN AUTHENTIC FRIEND OR TWO

Finally, it will not be enough to quietly replace stubborn old tools without enlisting the support of some other "real-life" people. You don't need a private one-man party; you need a group of cheerleaders to celebrate your victories and remind you that you are doing a good thing. Telling someone else that you are making some changes - even if it's embarrassing - will set you up for success, even during times when you don't feel like being successful.

The path to success will include many small failures and possibly even a few big ones. There will be times when you will need a friend in your corner to believe in you and encourage you, even when you don't believe in yourself.

At times we forget who we are and the person who we want to be. According to the old saying, "We judge other people by their actions, but ourselves by our own good intentions." It's easier for us to excuse our inconsistencies than it is for other people to accept them. Take advantage of that by making sure another set of eyes is watching you, another conscience is evaluating you and another supporter is believing in you.

Having a friend like that may feel like a crutch. It absolutely is! Unless you are perfect in every way you will always live with - and through - your personal brokenness. Crutches are for broken people, and that's each and every one of us. You might be stoic and go it alone without a crutch, but it seems pointless if the result is to sit in a corner and remain broken.

Replacing our blunt and broken tools will not only involve other people, but often the shiny new precision instruments we replace them with will be other people.

If we are designed to need each other, then a person void of quality relationships will always be looking to fill that vacuum with something counterfeit - some blunt, broken or ill-fitting junk. In the opening chapters of the Bible, God looks at the man who He walks and talks with daily in a garden paradise, and says that something is still lacking: "It is not good for the man to be alone" (Genesis 2:18, GW).

Are friendships a crutch? A better question is this:

"If I view friendships as a crutch and am too proud to take them up, what other crutch will I inevitably take up instead?"

Boris was a hopeless alcoholic, obsessed with finding a girlfriend and getting married. Although he was a likeable guy, his desperation to find a bride was a little too obvious. It seemed to go before him like a snowplough, sweeping any young ladies well away. Boris craved a relationship. He didn't really need a wife so badly; he just needed a few good friends. When he began attending a local church he was lucky enough to find some positive people who could love him for who he was. When he told them of his failures and alcoholism, they only seemed to respect and accept him even more.

Before long, with a few authentic friends in his life, Boris managed to put down the alcohol tool. Surprisingly, he didn't even seem to miss it. His desire to get married also took a more appropriate level of priority in his life and ceased to be a desperate and driving force.

When people find fulfilment in the authentic relationships they were born for, it's amazing what long-held dysfunctional tools they will freely put down.

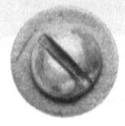

ALTERNATIVE

WHAT MIGHT OTHER PEOPLE USE INSTEAD OF YOUR TOOL TO ACHIEVE THE SAME POSITIVE OUTCOMES AS ABOVE?

REFLECTION

WHO DO YOU REALLY WANT TO BE LIKE, AND WHAT TOOLS DO PEOPLE YOU REALLY RESPECT USE TO ACHIEVE THEIR RESULTS?

REFLECTION

"WHO COULD I ASK TO HELP ME LEARN TO USE BETTER TOOLS?"

MY HOPE FOR YOU

Everybody deserves an exciting story like that; a rich, fulfilling and happy ending. I hope you will have the courage to take a sober and thorough look at yourself and the honesty to confess what your tools have cost across all of the dimensions of your life. I hope you will be filled with insight as you thirst for answers, and give yourself liberty to find them.

When you come to terms with your dysfunctional tools and their source I hope you are quick to forgive anyone who has wronged you, making you free to leave the past behind like never before.

My ultimate hope is that your journey into wholeness becomes a means of bringing others closer, liberating you from shame, withdrawal and loneliness, and bringing freedom for the true adventure which you were born for: relationships in which the real you is fully known and fully loved.

PHOTOCOPY THE FOLLOWING PAGES IN ORDER TO
EXPLORE OTHER TOOLS YOU WISH TO ADDRESS

NAME THE TOOL:

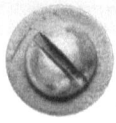

NEGATIVE

WHAT NEGATIVE EFFECTS IS THIS TOOL HAVING ON YOU?

POSITIVE

IN WHAT WAYS IS THIS TOOL DOING SOMETHING FOR YOU?

RETROSPECTIVE

WHAT IS YOUR FIRST MEMORY OF EVER PICKING UP THIS TOOL?

ALTERNATIVE

WHAT MIGHT OTHER PEOPLE USE INSTEAD OF YOUR TOOL TO ACHIEVE THE SAME POSITIVE OUTCOMES AS ABOVE?

REFLECTION

WHO DO YOU REALLY WANT TO BE LIKE, AND WHAT TOOLS DO PEOPLE YOU REALLY RESPECT USE TO ACHIEVE THEIR RESULTS?

REFLECTION

"WHO COULD I ASK TO HELP ME LEARN TO USE BETTER TOOLS?"

ENDNOTES

Berne, E. (1964). Games People Play, New York: Rove Press.

Cloud, H., & Townsend, J. (1992) Boundaries: When to say Yes, When to say No; to take control of your life, Grand Rapids, Michigan: Zondervan.

Eldridge, J. (2001). Wild at Heart, Nashville, Thomas Nelson

Houston, R. (2012). Unappreciated mothers resort to infidelity the day after Mother's Day, theexaminer.com, May 11, 2012

http://www.examiner.com/article/unappreciated-mothers-resort-to-infidelity-the-day-after-mother-s-day, downloaded June 21, 2013.

Mackay, H. (2010). What Makes Us Tick? Sydney, Hachette.

Safran Foer, J. (2013). How Not to be Alone, The New York Times online, June 8, 2013.

http://mobile.nytimes.com/2013/06/09/opinion/sunday/how-not-to-be-alone.html, downloaded June 20, 2013.

www.ingramcontent.com/pod-product-compliance
Lightning Source LLC
Chambersburg PA
CBHW032047290426
44110CB00012B/985